RETICULATED PYTHON CARE GUIDE

Choosing A Healthy Python, Optimal Substrate Choices, Meeting Nutritional Needs, Ideal Prey Size, Pet Interactions, And Understanding Age And Size

Ethan Harry

Table of Contents

CHAPTER ONE

INTRODUCTION TO RETICULATED PYTHONS

Overview Of Reticulated Pythons

Reticulated pythons (Python reticulatus) are among the longest snakes in the world, renowned for their extraordinary size and intricate patterns. The name "reticulated" derives from the Latin word "reticulatus," meaning net-like, which aptly describes the snake's complex and beautiful color patterns. These pythons are native to Southeast Asia, inhabiting countries such as Indonesia, Malaysia, the Philippines, and Thailand. Their habitats range from rainforests and woodlands to grasslands and nearby human settlements.

One of the most remarkable features of the reticulated python is its exceptional length.

Some individuals can exceed 20 feet, though the average length is typically between 10 to 15 feet. This substantial size makes them one of the longest snake species in the world. Despite their formidable length and girth, reticulated pythons are known for their agility. They are adept climbers and are often found in trees as well as on the ground. Their physical prowess enables them to navigate various terrains with ease.

Reticulated pythons have a varied diet that primarily consists of mammals and birds. They are ambush predators, relying on their excellent camouflage to blend into their surroundings. Once prey is within reach, the python strikes with remarkable speed, capturing its meal and using powerful constriction to subdue it. This method of hunting is highly effective and allows the python to take down prey significantly larger than itself.

In addition to their impressive physical attributes, reticulated pythons play a crucial role in their ecosystems. By controlling the populations of small to medium-sized mammals and birds, they help maintain a balanced environment. However, their interaction with humans can sometimes lead to conflicts, especially in areas where their natural habitats overlap with agricultural or residential zones.

Natural Habitat And Distribution

Reticulated pythons, known for their adaptability, thrive in a diverse range of habitats. These impressive snakes are commonly found in rainforests, woodlands, and grasslands, each providing unique resources and shelter. In the dense canopies of rainforests, reticulated pythons utilize the thick foliage for concealment and hunting. The woodlands offer a variety of ground cover and trees, facilitating their ambush predation techniques. Grasslands, with their open spaces, allow these pythons to bask and regulate their body temperature.

Beyond these natural habitats, reticulated pythons have shown remarkable adaptability to human-altered landscapes. They are frequently encountered in urban environments, agricultural areas, and coastal regions. Urban areas, with their plethora of rodents and other small mammals, provide ample food sources. Agricultural fields also offer abundant prey and the necessary cover for these stealthy predators. Coastal regions and mangroves, with their intricate water systems, are particularly favorable due to the python's affinity for water. These areas allow them to utilize their exceptional swimming abilities for hunting and escaping potential threats.

Water sources are a critical component of the reticulated python's habitat. Rivers, swamps, and other wetlands not only provide hydration but also serve as prime hunting grounds. These snakes are proficient swimmers and often pursue prey in and around water bodies, showcasing their versatility and predatory prowess.

The geographic distribution of reticulated pythons is extensive, spanning much of Southeast Asia. They inhabit numerous islands, including Sumatra, Borneo, and the Philippines, and are prevalent on the mainland in countries such as Thailand and Vietnam. This widespread distribution is a testament to their adaptability and resilience. Their ability to thrive in varied environments has enabled them to occupy a broad range across Southeast Asia, from dense jungles to bustling cities, illustrating their remarkable ecological versatility.

Physical Characteristics

The reticulated python's physical appearance is remarkably distinctive and captivating. These serpents possess a slender but muscular build, their bodies covered in smooth scales that form intricate patterns of geometric shapes. This complexity in patterning contributes to their striking appearance and serves a functional purpose. The coloration of reticulated pythons can vary widely, ranging from vibrant yellows and golds to more subdued browns and blacks. This diverse color palette allows them to blend seamlessly into their natural environments, providing effective camouflage that protects them from predators and enables them to ambush prey with precision.

A prominent feature of the reticulated python is its eyes, which bear a resemblance to those of cats due to their vertical slit pupils. This unique eye structure is specifically adapted for low-light conditions, making reticulated pythons formidable hunters during the dim light of dawn and dusk, as well as in the dead of night. These keen eyes enhance their ability to detect movement and potential prey in their surroundings, giving them a significant advantage in the wild.

Another fascinating aspect of the reticulated python's anatomy is its jaw structure. Unlike many other animals, reticulated pythons have highly flexible jaws. The presence of specialized ligaments allows their jawbones to separate, enabling them to open their mouths extraordinarily wide. This adaptability is crucial for their feeding habits, as it allows them to consume prey much larger than their head. This ability to swallow large prey whole is a hallmark of the python family and is essential for their survival, given their infrequent feeding schedule.

Behavior And Temperament

Reticulated pythons exhibit a range of behaviors and temperaments that can vary significantly depending on their environment and individual personality. In their natural habitat, these pythons are solitary creatures, interacting primarily during mating season. They are nocturnal hunters, utilizing their keen sense of smell and heat-sensing pits along their upper lip to locate warm-blooded prey.

Despite their reputation for aggression, reticulated pythons are not inherently hostile towards humans. Their perceived aggressiveness is often a defensive response to threats. In captivity, with proper handling and care, many reticulated pythons can become quite docile and tolerant of human interaction. However, their considerable size and strength necessitate experienced handlers who can provide an appropriate environment and respect their natural behaviors.

Reticulated pythons have a diverse diet, primarily consisting of mammals and birds. In the wild, they may prey on animals ranging from rodents and bats to larger mammals such as deer and pigs. Their powerful constriction method allows them to subdue prey efficiently, followed by swallowing it whole thanks to their highly flexible jaws.

Culturally, reticulated pythons hold significant importance in many regions where they are native. They feature prominently in local folklore and mythology, sometimes revered and other times feared. Their striking appearance and impressive size have also made them popular in the exotic pet trade. However, prospective owners must recognize the significant responsibilities that come with keeping such a large and powerful snake. Proper care, handling, and a suitable environment are crucial for the well-being of these majestic reptiles.

CHAPTER TWO

CHOOSING YOUR RETICULATED PYTHON

Selecting A Healthy Python

Selecting a healthy reticulated python is crucial for both the well-being of the animal and the owner's long-term satisfaction. To ensure your potential python is in good health, start by examining its physical appearance. Healthy pythons have clear, bright eyes, smooth and shiny scales, and a well-rounded body free from injuries or visible signs of disease. Any indication of dull or cloudy eyes outside of the shedding period could be a red flag.

Respiratory health is another critical factor. When examining the python, listen for any wheezing sounds and look for mucus around the nose or mouth, as these can be signs of respiratory infections. Open-mouth breathing is particularly concerning and should be addressed immediately, as respiratory infections are common in snakes but can become serious if left untreated.

Behavioral observation is equally important. A healthy python should be alert and responsive when handled. It should show a natural curiosity and move smoothly without appearing overly aggressive or unusually lethargic. Extreme aggression or lethargy can indicate underlying health issues or poor handling practices by the breeder or seller.

Checking for external parasites is another key step. Look closely around the eyes and under the scales for mites or ticks. These small pests can cause significant discomfort and health problems if not promptly treated. While external parasites are easier to spot, internal parasites are more elusive. Therefore, it's wise to have a veterinarian perform a thorough health check to rule out internal parasites and other potential health issues before making your purchase.

Breeder Vs. Pet Store: Where To Buy

Deciding where to buy your reticulated python is crucial, with breeders and pet stores offering distinct advantages and drawbacks.

Opting to buy from a reputable breeder is often the best choice for acquiring a healthy and well-cared-for python. Breeders usually possess extensive knowledge about the species and can provide detailed information about the python's health, lineage, and care history. They often specialize in specific morphs and can offer pythons with unique and desirable traits. Additionally, breeders tend to socialize their snakes from a young age, making them more accustomed to handling and interaction. This early socialization can lead to a more docile and manageable pet, enhancing your experience as an owner. Furthermore, breeders are typically passionate about their animals and committed to maintaining high standards of care and husbandry.

In contrast, pet stores can be more convenient and accessible, offering the advantage of immediate purchase without waiting for breeding seasons or availability.

However, the quality of care and knowledge can vary greatly between stores. Some pet stores may not provide the best environment or care for their reptiles, which can lead to health and behavioral issues down the line. It's not uncommon for pet store employees to lack the specialized knowledge that breeders have, potentially resulting in misinformation or inadequate care practices.

If you choose to buy from a pet store, thorough research is essential. Investigate the store's reputation and the condition of their animals. Look for signs of a healthy environment, such as clean enclosures and active, alert reptiles. Ask questions about the python's origin, age, and any health checks it has undergone. A reputable pet store should be transparent about their sourcing and care practices and be able to provide basic care information.

Age And Size Considerations

When selecting a reticulated python, it's important to consider the age and size of the snake. Juvenile pythons are often more adaptable to new environments and can be easier to handle and tame as they grow. These young snakes require significant care and attention, particularly during their early stages of development. This includes frequent feeding, monitoring for health issues, and ensuring their enclosure meets their growing needs. Juveniles are generally more flexible and can acclimate to new surroundings and handlers more readily, making them a good choice for those willing to invest time in their care.

On the other hand, adult pythons present a different set of considerations. While they are larger and can be more challenging to handle initially, they offer the advantage of having already reached a stable size. This can be appealing for those who wish to bypass the intensive care required for young pythons. Adult reticulated pythons have established temperaments, which can make their behavior more predictable. However, their size can be intimidating for some handlers, and they demand a more spacious and secure enclosure to accommodate their full-grown length and girth.

Reticulated pythons are among the largest snake species in the world, capable of reaching impressive lengths and requiring a long-term commitment. Prospective owners must be prepared for the substantial space and resources needed to house and care for a fully grown reticulated python. This includes ensuring adequate enclosure size, proper diet, and regular health check-ups. The commitment to their care extends for many years, as these snakes can live for several decades with proper care. Therefore, understanding the implications of their size and the care requirements for both juveniles and adults is crucial for anyone considering adding a reticulated python to their collection.

Understanding Morphs And Color Variants

Reticulated pythons are celebrated for their stunning variety of morphs and color variants, each offering a unique visual appeal. Morphs are genetic alterations that influence the coloration and patterning of a python's scales, creating a wide spectrum of possibilities. Among the most sought-after morphs are albino, tiger, and platinum, each distinguished by its own set of striking characteristics.

The albino morph is renowned for its lack of melanin, resulting in a python with a pale yellow or cream base color and bright orange or red accents. This morph's striking appearance makes it a favorite among enthusiasts. The tiger morph, on the other hand, features bold, contrasting stripes that resemble the stripes of a tiger, giving the python a distinctive and dramatic look. The platinum morph is characterized by its shimmering, metallic scales that give the python a sleek, silvery appearance.

When selecting a reticulated python, it's crucial to understand the various morphs and determine which one aligns with your preferences. Some morphs are more coveted and thus come with a higher price tag due to their rarity and the intricate breeding processes required to produce them. As a result, prices can vary significantly based on the morph's uniqueness and availability.

To ensure you acquire a healthy and authentic morph, it is essential to purchase from reputable breeders who specialize in reticulated pythons. Reputable breeders can provide detailed information about the morph's lineage and health, ensuring that you receive a python that meets your expectations both in terms of appearance and well-being

CHAPTER THREE

HOUSING AND ENCLOSURE SETUP

Enclosure Types And Sizes

Reticulated Pythons, being large and active snakes, necessitate spacious and secure enclosures to thrive. For a juvenile Reticulated Python, a terrarium measuring 4x2x2 feet is initially adequate. However, as the snake matures, it is crucial to upgrade to a larger habitat to accommodate its growth. Adult Reticulated Pythons require significantly more space, with an ideal enclosure size being 8x4x4 feet or larger. This spacious environment is essential to support their physical and mental well-being, providing ample room for movement, climbing, and exercise.

When selecting an enclosure, it is important to choose sturdy materials such as glass, plastic, or wood. Each material has its advantages. Glass enclosures offer excellent visibility and ease of cleaning, allowing you to observe your snake's behavior and maintain the habitat with minimal effort. On the other hand, plastic and wood enclosures can offer better insulation, helping to maintain a stable temperature and humidity level inside the habitat. Regardless of the material, the enclosure should be equipped with secure locking mechanisms to prevent escapes, as Reticulated Pythons are known for their ability to escape from poorly secured habitats.

Ventilation is another critical aspect of enclosure design. Proper airflow is necessary to prevent the buildup of stale air and excess humidity, which can lead to health issues for your snake. Ensure that the enclosure has adequate ventilation to maintain a healthy environment. In summary, a well-sized and properly constructed enclosure is vital for the health and well-being of your Reticulated Python, providing the space and conditions necessary for a happy and healthy life.

Substrate Options

Selecting the right substrate is crucial for ensuring hygiene and comfort in the enclosure of Reticulated Pythons. The substrate not only contributes to the aesthetic appeal of the habitat but also plays a significant role in maintaining appropriate humidity levels and ease of cleaning.

Aspen Bedding is a popular choice for Reticulated Pythons due to its absorbent properties and ease of maintenance. Made from shredded aspen wood, this substrate provides a natural appearance and is effective at absorbing excess moisture. This helps in controlling the humidity levels within the enclosure, which is essential for the health of the python. Additionally, aspen bedding is relatively easy to clean, making it a convenient option for pet owners who want to keep their python's habitat tidy with minimal effort.

Coconut Fiber, also known as coir, is another excellent substrate option. Coir is derived from the husks of coconuts and is known for its exceptional moisture-retention capabilities. This makes it ideal for creating a humid environment that mimics the python's natural habitat. Coconut fiber is biodegradable, which is an added benefit for environmentally conscious keepers. It also helps in maintaining the necessary humidity levels while being straightforward to clean. However, it may require more frequent replacement compared to other substrates.

Reptile Carpet offers a washable and reusable alternative. Made from synthetic fibers, reptile carpet is designed to be easy to clean and maintain. It helps in controlling odors and bacteria but may need regular washing to prevent build-up. While it's durable and cost-effective in the long run, some pet owners may find it requires more frequent upkeep compared to other substrates.

Heating And Lighting Requirements

Reticulated Pythons are ectothermic, meaning they depend on external heat sources to regulate their body temperature. Proper heating is crucial for their digestion and overall well-being. To create an optimal temperature gradient within their enclosure, follow these guidelines:

Heat Source: Implement an under-tank heater or heat lamp to establish a temperature gradient. The warm side of the enclosure should maintain a temperature between 85-90°F (29-32°C), while the cooler side should be kept around 75-80°F (24-27°C). This gradient allows the snake to thermoregulate effectively by moving between warmer and cooler areas according to its needs. Ensure that the heat source is positioned to provide these varying temperatures without creating hotspots.

Thermostat: Utilize a thermostat to regulate the heat source and prevent overheating. This device helps maintain a stable and consistent temperature within the enclosure, avoiding temperature fluctuations that can stress the snake. The thermostat should be connected to the heat source and set to the appropriate temperature range to ensure optimal conditions.

Lighting: Although Reticulated Pythons do not require UVB lighting, providing a light cycle that mimics natural day and night patterns can benefit their biological rhythms. A standard light bulb on a 12-hour on/12-hour off cycle generally suffices. This lighting setup helps simulate natural environmental changes and supports the snake's internal clock, which can improve its overall health and behavior.

Humidity Control

Humidity Control is essential for the health and well-being of Reticulated Pythons. Maintaining the right humidity levels in their enclosure is crucial for their shedding process and respiratory health. Ideally, the dry side of the enclosure should have a humidity level of 50-60%, while the humid side should range between 60-80%. This gradient allows the python to choose the environment that best suits its needs at any given time.

To achieve and manage these humidity levels, there are several strategies you can employ:

1. Water Dish: Provide a large, shallow water dish in the enclosure. This dish serves a dual purpose: it helps to maintain the overall humidity levels and provides the snake with a source of hydration. Ensure the dish is large enough for the snake to soak in, as this will also aid in the shedding process.

2. Humidity Hide: Incorporate a humidity hide into the enclosure by placing damp sphagnum moss or coconut fiber inside a hide box. This hide box should be positioned on the humid side of the enclosure. The moist substrate provides a retreat where the snake can seek comfort, especially when shedding. This setup helps to ensure that the snake can easily access a humid microenvironment when needed.

3.   Misting: Lightly mist the enclosure with water if you notice that the humidity levels are dropping. Regular monitoring with a hygrometer will help you keep track of the humidity levels. Be cautious not to over-mist, as excessive moisture can create an environment conducive to mold growth and respiratory issues. Proper ventilation is also important to prevent excess humidity from becoming a problem.

Enclosure Decorations And Hides

Providing appropriate decorations and hides in the enclosure helps replicate the snake's natural habitat and reduces stress. Here's what to consider:

Hides

Hides are essential for providing your reticulated python with a sense of security and comfort. It's important to include multiple hides in the enclosure, such as a warm hide and a cool hide, to offer the snake choices based on its temperature preference. These hides can be commercially available or homemade options using materials like plastic containers or logs. Positioning one hide in the warmer area and another in the cooler area allows the python to thermoregulate while feeling secure. The hides should be large enough for the snake to fit comfortably but snug enough to make it feel safe and enclosed.

Climbing Opportunities

Reticulated Pythons are excellent climbers and benefit greatly from vertical space in their enclosures. Providing branches, shelves, or climbing structures allows these snakes to engage in natural behaviors, promoting physical and mental well-being. When selecting climbing materials, ensure they are sturdy enough to support the weight of your python and are securely anchored to prevent accidents. Branches from safe trees or commercially available reptile climbing accessories can be used to create a stimulating environment.

Water Features

Adding a shallow water feature to the enclosure can offer enrichment and help maintain proper humidity levels. A large, shallow water dish can serve this purpose effectively, providing the python with the opportunity to soak if desired. Ensure the water is clean and changed regularly to prevent bacterial growth. The water feature should be easy to access but not so deep that it poses a drowning risk.

CHAPTER FOUR

DIET AND FEEDING

Nutritional Needs

Reticulated pythons are carnivorous reptiles that thrive on a diet primarily consisting of whole prey items. In their natural habitat, these pythons consume a diverse array of animals, including birds, mammals, and occasionally other reptiles. This varied diet is crucial for meeting their complex nutritional requirements. In captivity, it's essential to replicate their natural feeding habits to ensure they receive all the necessary nutrients for optimal health and well-being.

Whole prey items, such as rats, mice, and rabbits, are ideal for reticulated pythons. These prey items provide a balanced diet, containing the right proportions of protein, fat, vitamins, and minerals essential for the python's growth and maintenance. For instance, rodents like rats and mice are excellent sources of protein and fat, while rabbits offer a slightly leaner option, helping to diversify the nutrient intake. Each type of prey also contributes different vitamins and minerals, ensuring a comprehensive dietary profile.

It's important to avoid feeding reticulated pythons processed or prepared foods. Such foods often lack the essential nutrients found in whole prey and may lead to deficiencies or health issues over time. Processed foods can also contain additives and preservatives that might be harmful to the snake's health. Moreover, the act of consuming whole prey items provides not only the necessary nutrients but also stimulates natural hunting and feeding behaviors, contributing to the python's overall well-being.

Feeding frequency is another critical aspect of a reticulated python's nutritional care. Juveniles typically require more frequent feeding, about once a week, due to their rapid growth rates. Adults, on the other hand, may need to be fed less frequently, approximately every two to four weeks, depending on their size and activity level. Overfeeding can lead to obesity and related health issues, so it's important to monitor the snake's body condition and adjust feeding schedules accordingly.

Feeding Schedule By Age And Size

The feeding schedule for a reticulated python varies significantly based on its age and size, requiring careful adjustment to ensure optimal health and growth. Younger pythons, such as hatchlings and juveniles, need more frequent feeding than their adult counterparts. Hatchlings, for instance, should be fed every 5-7 days. This frequent feeding is necessary to support their rapid growth and high metabolic rate. Juveniles, which are slightly older, can be fed less frequently, approximately every 7-10 days. This gradual reduction in feeding frequency helps them transition smoothly as they mature.

As reticulated pythons grow and approach adulthood, their feeding requirements change. Adult pythons, having slower metabolic rates compared to their younger stages, typically need to be fed every 10-14 days. This reduced frequency is sufficient to maintain their body condition without the risk of overfeeding. For large, fully-grown adult reticulated pythons, the feeding interval can be extended even further. These mature individuals may only require feeding once every 2-3 weeks, as their slower metabolism and larger body size mean they can sustain themselves longer between meals.

It's crucial to monitor the python's body condition regularly and adjust the feeding schedule accordingly. Overfeeding can lead to obesity and associated health problems, while underfeeding can result in malnutrition and stunted growth. By observing the python's physical condition and response to feeding, keepers can ensure they are providing the appropriate amount of food. Additionally, the type of prey offered should be suitable for the python's size, as feeding prey that is too large or too small can also cause issues.

Prey Size And Type

Choosing the right prey size and type is crucial for the health and well-being of your reticulated python. Feeding prey that is too large can cause regurgitation and digestive issues, while prey that is too small may not provide adequate nutrition. As a general rule, the prey item should be no larger than the widest part of the python's body. This ensures that the python can safely swallow and digest the prey without complications.

For hatchlings and juvenile reticulated pythons, appropriately-sized mice or rat pups are ideal. These smaller prey items are easy for young pythons to consume and provide the necessary nutrients for their growth and development. As the python grows, the size of the prey should increase accordingly. This gradual increase helps the python adapt to larger prey and ensures they receive the right amount of nutrition.

Adult reticulated pythons can handle much larger prey. Depending on the size of the python, adult rats, rabbits, or even small pigs can be suitable food sources. It is essential to monitor the python's feeding response and adjust the prey size as needed. Overfeeding or offering prey that is too large can lead to health issues, so careful observation is necessary.

Offering a variety of prey types can also be beneficial. Different prey items provide nutritional diversity, which can help maintain the python's health. However, it is important to ensure that all prey offered is safe and appropriate for the python's size. Avoid feeding wild-caught prey, as they can carry diseases or parasites that could harm the python.

Feeding Techniques And Tips

Feeding a reticulated python requires careful attention to techniques and tips to ensure the process is both safe and effective. One of the primary tools to use during feeding is feeding tongs or forceps. These tools are essential for presenting prey to the python, significantly reducing the risk of accidental bites. By using tongs, you help the python associate the feeding response with the tongs rather than your hands, which can prevent potential misunderstandings and bites in the future.

Feeding the python in its enclosure is generally recommended. This practice minimizes stress on the snake and reduces the likelihood of regurgitation, which can occur if the python is handled immediately after eating. When feeding with frozen prey, it's crucial to thaw it completely and then warm it to a temperature slightly above room temperature. This makes the prey more appealing to the python and simulates the warmth of a live animal, encouraging a strong feeding response.

After feeding, it's essential to avoid handling the python for at least 24-48 hours. This period allows the snake to properly digest its meal without the added stress of being handled. Handling too soon after feeding can lead to regurgitation, which is not only unpleasant but can also be harmful to the snake's health.

Additionally, always monitor the python during feeding to ensure it is eating properly and that there are no issues with the prey item being too large or the snake having difficulty swallowing. If any problems arise, it's important to address them promptly to prevent potential health issues. Regular feeding schedules and proper prey size according to the python's age and size are also crucial for maintaining the snake's health and well-being.

Handling Feeding Issues

Feeding issues can sometimes arise with reticulated pythons, and addressing them promptly is crucial to maintain their health. One common issue is a refusal to eat, which can stem from several factors including stress, illness, improper husbandry, or inappropriate prey size. To resolve this, first ensure the python's enclosure conditions are optimal. This includes maintaining the correct temperature and humidity levels, providing hiding spots, and minimizing stress factors. If the python refuses to eat, try offering different prey types or sizes, or present the prey in a different manner, such as leaving it in the enclosure overnight. Sometimes, live prey can stimulate feeding responses in reluctant eaters, but be cautious as live prey can injure your python. If the python continues to refuse food despite these adjustments, it is advisable to consult a reptile veterinarian to rule out any underlying health problems.

Another issue that may arise is regurgitation, which is often caused by handling the python too soon after feeding or feeding prey that is too large. To prevent this, ensure that the python is not disturbed for at least 24-48 hours after a meal. During this period, avoid handling or any other activities that might stress the python. Always select prey that is appropriately sized, generally no larger than the widest part of the python's body. If regurgitation persists, it is essential to seek veterinary advice promptly. Chronic regurgitation can lead to dehydration and other serious health complications, so early intervention is critical.

CHAPTER FIVE

HANDLING AND SOCIALIZATION

Safe Handling Practices

Handling a reticulated python requires careful attention to safety to ensure the well-being of both you and the snake. Here are some fundamental practices to follow:

Preparation: Before handling, it's crucial to make sure your python is aware of your presence. Gently tap the enclosure to alert the snake, reducing the chance of startling it. This helps the python understand that it's time for interaction, not feeding, thereby minimizing the risk of defensive reactions.

Support the Body: When picking up the python, always support the full length of its body. Use both hands, placing one hand near the head and the other supporting the midsection. Never lift the snake by its tail or head alone, as this can cause injury or stress. Proper support ensures the snake feels secure and helps prevent it from wriggling out of your grip.

Firm but Gentle Grip: Maintain a firm yet gentle grip. Reticulated pythons are strong and can exert considerable pressure, but using excessive force can stress or injure the snake. A firm hold prevents the python from slipping, while a gentle approach ensures its comfort and reduces the risk of defensive behavior.

Avoiding the Head: Refrain from touching the snake's head, as this can provoke defensive behavior. Instead, approach the python from the side or underneath, minimizing the likelihood of being mistaken for prey. Reticulated pythons may react defensively if they feel threatened, especially when their head is touched unexpectedly.

Handling Time: Limit handling sessions to 15-20 minutes initially, gradually increasing the duration as the snake becomes more accustomed to you. Frequent, short handling sessions are better than infrequent, long ones. This allows the python to build trust and become more comfortable with handling over time.

Socialization Techniques

Socializing a reticulated python involves acclimating it to human interaction and reducing stress during handling. Effective techniques for achieving this goal are essential for a harmonious relationship between the snake and its handler.

First, establish a consistent routine for handling and feeding. Snakes thrive on predictability, and a regular schedule helps them feel secure. Handling the snake at the same time each day can create a sense of familiarity and safety. This predictability reduces stress and makes the snake more receptive to socialization efforts.

Second, ensure a calm and quiet environment during handling sessions. Sudden movements or loud noises can startle the snake, hindering the socialization process. A serene atmosphere allows the python to feel more at ease, making it easier for it to become accustomed to human interaction.

Third, employ positive reinforcement techniques. Offering food rewards after successful handling sessions can help the snake associate handling with positive experiences. This method encourages the snake to view human interaction as beneficial, fostering a more trusting relationship. For example, offering a small treat or a favorite food item can reinforce good behavior and reduce anxiety during handling.

Gradual desensitization is another crucial technique. Introduce your python to new stimuli and environments slowly and carefully. Start with familiar settings and gradually expand to different rooms or outdoor areas, weather permitting. This gradual exposure helps the snake become more adaptable and less fearful of new experiences.

Lastly, remember that socializing a reticulated python takes time and patience. Consistent, gentle handling will build trust and reduce stress over time. It's important to be patient and persistent, as rushing the process can be counterproductive. Regular, calm interactions will eventually lead to a more confident and well-socialized python.

Recognizing Stress And Aggression

Understanding how to recognize stress and aggression in pythons is essential for ensuring their well-being and safe handling. Various signs can indicate that a python is feeling threatened or agitated.

Hissing is one of the most common indicators of discomfort. When a python hisses, it is signaling that it feels threatened and is warning you to keep your distance. It is crucial to respect this signal and avoid further handling until the snake calms down.

Coiling is another behavior to watch for. If a python coils tightly around your arm or hand, it may be feeling threatened or stressed. Gently and carefully uncoil the snake and return it to its enclosure to help alleviate its discomfort.

Striking is a more aggressive behavior and a clear sign that the python is feeling defensive. If the snake strikes, it is best to avoid handling it and allow it some time to relax. Handling should be minimal until the snake exhibits more relaxed behavior.

Rapid Breathing can be a sign of stress. If you notice the python's breathing becoming quick and heavy, it may be experiencing anxiety. Reducing handling time and ensuring the enclosure's environment is comfortable can help mitigate this stress.

Muscle Tension is another key sign of a stressed python. A snake that is tense and has a rigid body is on high alert and may react unpredictably. Handle it with extreme care, and avoid any sudden movements that could further agitate it.

Interaction With Other Pets

Introducing a reticulated python to other pets requires careful consideration and vigilant supervision. The large size and predatory nature of reticulated pythons mean that interactions with other animals should be handled with extreme caution. Here are essential guidelines for ensuring a safe and stress-free environment for all pets involved.

Supervised Interactions: Always supervise any interaction between your python and other pets. Never leave them alone together, as accidents can happen quickly due to the python's size and hunting instincts. Close supervision helps prevent potential harm to either animal and ensures that any signs of distress or aggression are promptly addressed.

Separate Enclosures: To prevent stress and possible injuries, it is crucial to keep the python's enclosure separate from that of other pets. A distinct, secure habitat for each animal reduces the risk of accidental contact and ensures that the python's presence does not unduly affect the well-being of other pets.

Calm Introduction: If you choose to introduce your python to other pets, do so gradually and in a controlled setting. Begin by allowing the animals to observe each other from a safe distance. This method helps minimize stress and allows both the python and the other pets to acclimate to each other's presence without direct interaction.

Monitor Reactions: Pay close attention to the reactions of both the python and the other pets during introductions. Watch for any signs of stress, aggression, or fear. If either animal shows signs of discomfort or hostility, it is vital to separate them immediately to avoid any potential conflicts or injuries.

Safety First: The safety and well-being of all pets should be your top priority. If there is any uncertainty regarding the safety of interactions, it is best to avoid them altogether. Ensuring a harmonious environment for all your pets requires patience and careful management.

Bonding With Your Python

Building a strong bond with your reticulated python is essential for both its well-being and your enjoyment as a keeper. Trust and reduced stress come from consistent and positive interactions. Here's how you can nurture this relationship:

Regular Handling: Engage in consistent, gentle handling sessions. Start with short periods and gradually increase as the python becomes more comfortable. Gentle, calm touches help the python become accustomed to your presence and touch. Avoid sudden movements that could startle it.

Feeding Rituals: Establish a regular feeding routine. Incorporate positive interactions during feeding times, and consider hand-feeding if feasible. This creates a positive association between you and the python, making it more likely to view you as a source of comfort rather than a threat.

Environmental Enrichment: Enhance the python's enclosure with environmental enrichment. Add climbing branches, hiding spots, and water features. A stimulating environment not only keeps the python physically active but also mentally engaged, contributing to its overall well-being. An enriched habitat can make your python more relaxed and receptive to interaction.

Respecting Boundaries: Always respect your python's boundaries. If the python shows signs of stress or discomfort, such as hissing or defensive postures, avoid handling it at that time. Building trust requires understanding and respecting its needs and comfort levels. Patience is key in creating a bond where the python feels safe and secure.

Observation: Spend time observing your python in its enclosure without direct interaction. This allows you to learn about its behavior and preferences, which can help tailor your interactions to better suit its needs. Observing how it responds to different stimuli provides valuable insights into its comfort and stress levels, further strengthening your bond.

CHAPTER SIX

HEALTH AND WELLNESS

Common Health Issues

Reticulated pythons, known for their impressive size and strength, are generally hardy reptiles, but they can face health challenges if their care isn't optimized. Among the most common health issues are respiratory infections, scale rot, and metabolic bone disease.

Respiratory infections in reticulated pythons often arise due to inadequate humidity or improper heating within their habitat. These infections can be signaled by several symptoms: wheezing or labored breathing, nasal discharge, and open-mouth breathing. Maintaining appropriate humidity levels and ensuring that the heating elements in the enclosure are functioning correctly can help prevent these issues. If an infection does occur, prompt veterinary attention is crucial to avoid more serious complications. Scale rot is another concern, usually resulting from excessive moisture and poor hygiene in the snake's enclosure. This condition manifests as discolored, swollen, or damaged scales and can progress to more severe infections if not addressed. To prevent scale rot, it is essential to keep the enclosure clean and dry, monitor humidity levels closely, and provide proper ventilation.

Metabolic bone disease (MBD) is a serious condition stemming from a deficiency in calcium and vitamin D3, which are crucial for maintaining healthy bone structure. MBD leads to weakened bones, making them soft or deformed, and can cause significant mobility issues for the python. Ensuring a proper diet rich in calcium and vitamin D3, along with exposure to UVB lighting, can help prevent this disease. If signs of MBD are noticed, such as difficulty moving or bone deformities, seeking veterinary care is important to manage and treat the condition effectively.

Parasites And Infections

Pythons, like many reptiles, can be susceptible to a variety of parasites and infections, which require vigilant management to ensure their health and well-being.

External Parasites: Among the most common external parasites are mites and ticks. Mites are particularly problematic for pythons, as they cause intense irritation and can lead to secondary infections if not promptly addressed. Affected pythons may exhibit symptoms such as excessive rubbing against objects or surfaces, and visible mites may be observed on the skin. These external parasites can be challenging to eliminate, and thorough cleaning and appropriate treatment are crucial to manage an infestation.

Internal Parasites: Internal parasites, including worms and protozoa, can affect a python's digestive system, leading to various health issues. Symptoms of internal parasitism often include weight loss, a diminished appetite, and abnormal feces. Regular fecal examinations are essential for early detection and treatment of internal parasites. Early intervention can prevent more severe health problems and ensure the python remains healthy.

Infections: Pythons can also suffer from bacterial and fungal infections, which are often linked to poor husbandry practices. These infections can manifest in several ways, including skin lesions, abnormal shedding patterns, and general lethargy. Proper husbandry, including maintaining appropriate humidity levels and cleanliness in the python's habitat, is critical in preventing these infections. Addressing any signs of infection promptly with veterinary care is important to prevent the spread of illness and to support the python's recovery.

Signs Of Illness

Identifying the signs of illness in your pet is essential for ensuring their well-being and administering prompt treatment. Early detection often leads to more effective care, so it's important to be vigilant about any changes in your pet's behavior or physical state.

Behavioral Changes: One of the first indicators of illness is a change in behavior. Pets that are unwell may become more reclusive than usual. If your pet is spending excessive time hiding, displaying unusual lethargy, or showing a marked reluctance to engage in normal activities, these can be signs that something is wrong. Behavioral shifts, such as increased aggression or irritability, can also indicate discomfort or distress.

Physical Changes: Regular observation of your pet's physical appearance is vital. Look for any noticeable abnormalities such as swelling, discoloration, or the presence of sores. Changes in the skin and scales can also be telling. For example, if you notice abnormal shedding, unusual texture, or changes in coloration, these could be symptoms of a health issue. Pay attention to any asymmetrical growths or lesions, which can indicate underlying problems.

Eating Habits: An abrupt change in eating habits is another critical sign of illness. A sudden loss of appetite or difficulty in swallowing can be red flags that your pet is experiencing health issues. It's important to monitor their feeding patterns closely. A decrease in food intake or a refusal to eat can signal a range of problems, from minor digestive issues to more serious conditions that require veterinary attention.

Preventative health care is crucial in ensuring the well-being of your Reticulated Python. By adhering to a few essential practices, you can significantly reduce the risk of health issues and promote a long, healthy life for your snake.

Enclosure Maintenance: The cleanliness and environmental conditions of your python's enclosure are fundamental to its health. Regularly clean and disinfect the habitat to prevent the buildup of harmful bacteria and parasites. Ensure that the enclosure maintains the proper humidity and temperature levels, as these factors are critical for your python's physiological functions. Regularly check for and remove any waste or uneaten food, and replace substrate as needed to keep the habitat hygienic and comfortable.

Diet and Nutrition: Providing a balanced diet tailored to your python's size, age, and dietary needs is vital for its health. Feed your Reticulated Python appropriately sized prey items to prevent obesity and nutritional deficiencies. Proper nutrition supports overall health and helps prevent conditions such as metabolic bone disease, which can result from improper diet. Always ensure that the prey items are appropriately thawed and free of contaminants to avoid introducing potential health risks.

Regular Health Checks: Conduct regular visual inspections of your python to monitor its health. Look for signs of illness or injury, such as changes in behavior, unusual shedding patterns, or physical abnormalities. A healthy Reticulated Python will have clear eyes, smooth, well-hydrated scales, and will be active and alert. Early detection of potential health issues allows for prompt intervention, which can be crucial for effective treatment.

Finding A Reptile Veterinarian

Finding a qualified reptile veterinarian is crucial for addressing health issues and providing emergency care for your Reticulated Python. Here's a guide to help you find the right professional:

Specialization: When searching for a reptile veterinarian, prioritize those who specialize in reptiles or exotics. These veterinarians possess the specific knowledge and expertise required to manage the unique health needs of Reticulated Pythons. A specialist will be well-versed in the proper care, treatment, and medical procedures suited to this particular species, ensuring your python receives the best possible care.

Referrals and Reviews: Seeking recommendations from other reptile owners can be an effective way to find a reputable veterinarian. Engage with local reptile clubs, online forums, or social media groups dedicated to reptile care. Experienced reptile owners often share their experiences and can point you towards trusted professionals. Additionally, online reviews and ratings can offer insights into the quality of care provided by different veterinarians. Look for feedback that highlights positive experiences with reptile-specific care, as well as comments on the vet's communication and professionalism.

Initial Consultation: Before committing to a veterinarian, schedule an initial consultation. This meeting provides an opportunity to discuss your Reticulated Python's specific needs and observe the vet's familiarity with the species. During the consultation, inquire about their experience with Reticulated Pythons, their approach to care, and their availability for emergencies. Assessing the veterinarian's approach and demeanor during this visit will help you gauge their expertise and the level of care they offer. It's essential that you feel confident in their ability to provide the best care for your python.

☐

CHAPTER SEVEN

BREEDING RETICULATED PYTHONS

Breeding Age And Size

Reticulated Pythons achieve sexual maturity based on a combination of age, size, and overall health. Generally, females become ready to breed between 3 to 4 years of age, while males often reach maturity slightly earlier, around 2 to 3 years old. However, size is a more reliable indicator of readiness than age alone. Females should be at least 8 to 10 feet long and weigh approximately 15 to 20 pounds before they are considered suitable for breeding. Males, while they can be smaller, must be in robust health and fully grown to ensure effective reproduction.

Before initiating the breeding process, it is crucial to verify that both snakes are in peak condition. This means providing them with a well-balanced diet and maintaining optimal husbandry practices. Good health is essential not only for successful mating but also for the overall well-being of the reptiles. Ensuring that the snakes are free from parasites and illnesses is imperative to avoid complications during both the breeding process and the incubation of eggs.

Proper preparation involves more than just meeting size and age criteria; it includes ensuring that the environment supports their health and reproductive needs. This means maintaining proper temperature, humidity, and cleanliness in their habitat. A healthy, well-cared-for Reticulated

Python pair will be more likely to achieve successful breeding outcomes, leading to a smoother incubation period and better survival rates for the hatchlings.

Breeding Behavior

Breeding behavior in Reticulated Pythons involves several stages, beginning with courtship and leading to mating. During courtship, males engage in a behavior known as "tail wagging." This involves rubbing their tails against the female's body, which serves to stimulate her and prepare her for mating. This tail rubbing can last from several hours to several days, depending on the receptiveness of the female. If she responds positively, the mating process will follow.

Mating in Reticulated Pythons involves a specific alignment of the bodies. The male will align his body with the female's and perform "hemipenis insertion," where he uses one of his paired hemipenes to insert into the female's cloaca. This process is critical for fertilization, and it may need to be repeated several times to increase the chances of successful fertilization.

After mating, careful monitoring of both snakes is essential. The female will enter a pre-laying period, characterized by increased reclusiveness and a tendency to spend more time in her hiding spots. This period requires special attention to environmental conditions. Proper temperature and humidity levels are crucial to support the female's reproductive process. Maintaining these conditions helps ensure that the female remains healthy and capable of laying eggs.

Egg Incubation

Once a female Reticulated Python lays her eggs, typically after a gestation period of approximately 90 days, meticulous care is essential for successful incubation. Reticulated Python eggs have a leathery shell, which necessitates a carefully controlled incubation environment to prevent them from drying out.

To ensure optimal conditions, it is crucial to use a reliable incubator capable of maintaining a stable temperature between 88 to 90 degrees Fahrenheit. This temperature range is critical as it supports the proper development of the embryos inside the eggs. Additionally, high humidity levels are vital, ideally maintained between 80% to 90%, to prevent the eggs from desiccating.

The eggs should be placed in a container filled with a moisture-retentive substrate, such as damp vermiculite or perlite. This substrate helps maintain the necessary humidity while preventing excessive moisture, which could lead to mold growth. Regular monitoring of the eggs is essential. Inspect them frequently for any signs of mold, decay, or other issues that could compromise their development.

Maintaining a consistent incubation environment is crucial for successful hatching. Fluctuations in temperature or humidity can adversely affect the development of the embryos. The incubation period for Reticulated Python eggs generally lasts between 80 to 90 days. As the eggs approach the end of this period, you will notice signs of hatching readiness, such as increased movement within the eggs.

Hatchling Care

Upon hatching, Reticulated Python hatchlings are in a delicate state and require meticulous care. The initial step involves gently transferring them from the incubator to a separate, carefully set-up enclosure. This new environment should be designed to meet the specific needs of these vulnerable young pythons.

A suitable enclosure for hatchlings must be small and secure to prevent escapes and to ensure they feel safe. Maintaining the right temperature and humidity is crucial for their well-being. The ideal temperature range for hatchlings is between 80 to 85 degrees Fahrenheit. Humidity should be high to aid in their first shed and help them acclimate to their new surroundings. Ensure the enclosure is equipped with hiding spots to offer the hatchlings a sense of security and reduce stress. A shallow water dish is also essential to provide hydration and help with shedding.

Feeding hatchlings requires careful attention to their size and nutritional needs. Offer small prey items, such as pinky mice, that are appropriately sized for their current growth stage. Hatchlings should be fed every 5 to 7 days. It's important to monitor their growth and health closely, ensuring they are growing consistently before introducing larger prey. Regular check-ups will help identify any potential health issues early and ensure the hatchlings are developing properly.

Ethical Breeding Practices

Ethical breeding practices are crucial for ensuring the health and well-being of Reticulated Pythons and their offspring. Breeding should be approached with a commitment to the long-term welfare of these reptiles. One fundamental aspect is to avoid breeding individuals with known health issues or genetic defects. Such practices can lead to serious health problems in the offspring, affecting their quality of life and overall well-being.

Equally important is being aware of market demand and avoiding overbreeding. Overbreeding can contribute to an oversupply of animals in the pet trade, which can lead to increased stress on the species and strain on animal shelters and rescue organizations. Breeding should be conducted thoughtfully, with consideration for the broader impact on the population and the resources available for their care.

Providing proper care and suitable living conditions for both the breeding pair and their offspring is another critical component of ethical breeding. Ensuring that the breeding pair has a clean, appropriately sized enclosure and access to proper nutrition and veterinary care is essential. The same level of care should be extended to the hatchlings, with appropriate habitats, food, and health monitoring.

Finally, having a well-considered plan for finding responsible homes for the hatchlings is vital. Potential owners should be thoroughly vetted to ensure they are prepared to provide a suitable environment for the snakes. By adhering to these ethical standards, breeders can contribute to the health of the species and support the responsible breeding community. Ethical practices not only enhance the welfare of Reticulated Pythons but also promote the integrity of the reptile breeding industry.

CHAPTER EIGHT

ENRICHMENT AND MENTAL STIMULATION

Importance Of Enrichment

Enrichment is a critical component in ensuring the well-being of captive reticulated pythons. In their natural habitat, these snakes are dynamic predators and explorers. They traverse diverse terrains to hunt for food, evade potential threats, and find suitable shelter. Their environment is rich with sensory stimuli that cater to their instinctual needs and behaviors. However, when kept in captivity, reticulated pythons can face a lack of stimulation, leading to boredom and stress if their enclosure does not offer a varied and engaging environment.

The significance of enrichment lies in its ability to replicate the complexities of a python's natural habitat. By incorporating elements that encourage climbing, foraging, and exploration, caretakers can help mimic the challenges these snakes would encounter in the wild. This approach not only reduces stress but also promotes overall health and well-being. Enrichment activities might include adding varied substrates, providing hiding spots, incorporating branches or logs for climbing, and offering food in a manner that stimulates natural hunting behaviors.

Moreover, enrichment is vital in preventing behavioral issues that stem from monotony. Reticulated pythons are highly intelligent and require mental stimulation to remain active and engaged. Without adequate enrichment, they may display repetitive behaviors, such as incessant pacing or refusal to eat, which are often signs of stress or discomfort. These behaviors can indicate that the snake is not receiving the mental or physical stimulation it needs.

Types Of Enrichment Activities

Enrichment activities are crucial for the well-being of reticulated pythons, as they help mimic natural behaviors and enhance their quality of life. There are several types of enrichment that can be implemented:

Environmental Enrichment involves modifying the python's habitat to encourage natural behaviors. By adding elements such as branches, rocks, and climbing structures, you create an environment that mirrors the complexity of their natural habitat. This setup promotes climbing, exploring, and hiding, essential activities that contribute to the snake's physical and mental stimulation.

Sensory Enrichment focuses on stimulating the snake's senses. Introducing varied substrates like sand, soil, or bark can provide different tactile experiences. Additionally, using scents from prey items or other novel odors can engage the python's sense of smell, encouraging them to explore and investigate their surroundings more actively. These sensory changes help simulate the diverse experiences they might encounter in the wild.

Food Enrichment aims to replicate the effort involved in hunting and foraging. Offering food in various ways can stimulate the snake's predatory instincts. For example, hiding prey items within the enclosure or using puzzle feeders can challenge the python to work for its meal. This not only provides physical exercise but also mental stimulation, as it mimics the natural hunting process.

Interactive Enrichment includes activities that involve direct interaction with humans. While reticulated pythons are not usually handled frequently, occasional interactions can be beneficial. Using feeding tongs or introducing new, safe objects into the enclosure can provide the snake with new experiences and mental challenges. These interactions offer a change from their routine and can keep the python engaged and mentally stimulated.

Enhancing the habitat of your reticulated python with DIY enrichment can be both simple and cost-effective, while promoting natural behaviors and mental stimulation. Here are some easy-to-implement ideas:

1. Hide and Seek: Create a stimulating environment by placing food items in various hiding spots within the enclosure. Use cardboard boxes, logs, or artificial plants to conceal the food. This activity engages the snake's sense of smell and problem-solving abilities, encouraging it to explore and hunt.

2. Climbing Structures: Incorporate climbing elements like branches, driftwood, or PVC pipes into the enclosure. Ensure that these structures are securely anchored to prevent accidents. Climbing

helps the python stay physically active and mimics its natural habitat, promoting exercise and enrichment.

3. Varied Substrates: Regularly rotate different types of substrates to alter the texture of the enclosure floor. Mixing sand, soil, and leaves can offer new tactile experiences and prevent boredom. This change in environment keeps the enclosure interesting and stimulates the python's sensory exploration.

4. Scent Trails: Enhance the snake's natural hunting instincts by creating scent trails within the enclosure. Rub a prey item or food on various surfaces, leaving a trail that the python can follow. This encourages the snake to use its keen sense of smell to track down food, simulating a more natural foraging experience.

5. Safe Toys: Introduce non-toxic, safe toys that the python can explore. Simple items like cardboard tubes or soft balls can provide mental stimulation. Ensure that any toys are free from small parts or harmful materials to prevent any risk to the snake.

Monitoring And Adjusting Enrichment

Monitoring and adjusting enrichment activities for your reticulated python is crucial for ensuring their well-being and mental stimulation. Regular observation is key to understanding how your python interacts with enrichment items and whether these activities are fulfilling their intended purpose. Begin by noting how your snake engages with the various enrichment tools and activities you provide. Look for signs of engagement such as exploration, manipulation of objects, or increased activity levels. Conversely, if your python displays signs of stress, disinterest, or consistently ignores the enrichment items, it may indicate that adjustments are needed.

To maintain an enriching environment, it's essential to regularly change the type and placement of enrichment items. This approach helps prevent boredom and keeps the python mentally stimulated. For example, rotating different types of enrichment, such as hiding spots, climbing structures, or scent trails, can provide varied sensory experiences and keep your snake curious and active. Additionally, consider altering the location of these items within the enclosure to create new challenges and encourage exploration.

Tracking the python's responses to different enrichment activities can provide valuable insights into their preferences and needs. Pay attention to which activities seem to capture their interest and which ones they may avoid. This information is vital for tailoring enrichment strategies to suit your python's individual tastes and behaviors. By regularly adjusting enrichment based on your observations, you can create a dynamic and engaging environment that supports your reticulated python's physical and psychological well-being.

CHAPTER NINE

SEASONAL CARE CONSIDERATIONS

Seasonal Changes And Their Impact

Reticulated Pythons, native to tropical climates, thrive in stable, warm environments. However, their care in captivity often involves exposure to seasonal changes, particularly in temperate regions where temperatures fluctuate significantly. These seasonal variations can impact their metabolism, behavior, and overall health.

In their natural habitat, Reticulated Pythons experience a relatively constant climate. In captivity, though, they may encounter seasonal changes that can affect their activity levels and appetite. During colder months, temperatures drop, leading to a slowdown in their metabolic rate. As a result, your python may exhibit reduced activity and decreased appetite. This period of lower energy consumption is a natural response to cooler conditions, as their bodies adapt to conserve energy.

Conversely, during warmer months, temperatures rise, stimulating increased metabolic activity. This can result in heightened activity levels and a greater appetite. Your python may become more active, exploring its enclosure more frequently and showing increased interest in food. These changes in behavior and appetite are typical responses to warmer conditions and should be anticipated.

To ensure your Reticulated Python remains healthy throughout the year, it's crucial to monitor these seasonal changes closely. Adjustments to their care, such as modifying their enclosure's temperature and providing appropriate dietary adjustments, can help accommodate their needs. Proper heating and cooling systems are essential to maintain a stable environment that mimics their natural habitat as closely as possible.

Brumation In Reticulated Pythons

Brumation is a period of reduced metabolic activity in reptiles that typically occurs in response to cooler temperatures. While it is more commonly observed in temperate species, Reticulated Pythons in captivity can also undergo a form of brumation, especially when ambient temperatures drop significantly.

During brumation, your Reticulated Python's activity levels will decrease notably. You may observe your python spending more time hiding and being less responsive. This natural behavior is a survival adaptation to conserve energy when environmental conditions are not optimal. Despite this, it is crucial to maintain a suitable temperature range within the python's enclosure throughout this period. A gradual, controlled drop in temperature is essential; sudden or extreme changes can stress the animal and lead to health issues.

To effectively manage brumation, it is advisable to reduce the frequency of feedings and provide smaller meals. The python's digestive system will slow down during this time, and offering large or frequent meals could lead to gastrointestinal problems. Ensure that the enclosure includes a temperature gradient, allowing the python to move to warmer areas if necessary. Proper hydration is also vital, so make sure your python always has access to fresh water.

Monitor your python closely for any signs of distress or prolonged inactivity beyond what is typical for brumation. Maintaining regular health checks and consulting with a reptile veterinarian if any unusual symptoms arise will help ensure your python remains in good condition during this period.

Adjusting Care During Seasonal Transitions

As seasons shift, from winter to spring or summer to fall, it's essential to adjust your python's care routine to accommodate changing environmental conditions. Pythons, like other reptiles, are sensitive to temperature and humidity fluctuations, which can impact their health and behavior.

Start by gradually adjusting the heating elements in the enclosure to mirror the natural temperature variations of your python's native habitat. This gradual change helps prevent sudden stress and allows your python to acclimate smoothly to the new conditions. For instance, as temperatures rise in the spring and summer, you may need to lower the temperature of the heating elements.

Conversely, as temperatures drop in the fall and winter, increase the heat to maintain a warm environment.

During these seasonal transitions, closely observe your python's behavior and health. Pay attention to any changes in eating habits, shedding patterns, or activity levels, as these can be indicators of discomfort or stress. For example, if you notice reduced appetite or difficulty shedding, you may need to adjust the humidity levels in the enclosure. Higher humidity levels during warmer months can help prevent dehydration and facilitate proper shedding, while lower humidity levels in cooler months might be necessary to avoid excessive moisture buildup.

Preparing For Breeding Season

Preparing for the breeding season of Reticulated Pythons is crucial for a successful reproductive process. This season typically begins with cooler temperatures and increased humidity, replicating the natural environmental changes that trigger breeding behaviors in the wild.

To start, ensure both the male and female pythons are healthy and have reached sexual maturity. Proper nutrition and hydration are vital for their reproductive health. Monitor their weight regularly and adjust their diet to ensure they are in peak condition for breeding. Pythons that are well-fed and healthy are more likely to successfully reproduce.

As the breeding season approaches, gradually lower the temperature in the enclosure to mimic the natural seasonal cooling. This drop in temperature can help stimulate the pythons' reproductive behaviors. Additionally, provide suitable nesting sites within the enclosure and maintain high humidity levels. These conditions are crucial for supporting successful egg development and ensuring that the female has a comfortable environment to lay her eggs.

When breeding Reticulated Pythons, be prepared for the incubation period, which is a delicate phase requiring close monitoring. Reticulated Python eggs need a stable, warm environment to incubate effectively. Investing in a quality incubator is recommended if you plan to breed your pythons regularly. An incubator will help maintain the consistent temperature and humidity levels necessary for the eggs to develop properly.

THE END

www.ingramcontent.com/pod-product-compliance
Lightning Source LLC
Chambersburg PA
CBHW061059250726
48653CB00001B/480